ART OF TAT

A step by tatting design

copyright@2023

Sonia Wilson

Chapter One 3
  TATTING 3
Chapter Two 14
  Hand Positions 14
Chapter Three 28
  Rings and Picots 28

Chapter One

TATTING

Tatting, also known as frivolite in French, first appeared in Europe in the latter half of the eighteenth century. It is the craft of creating fine lace edges and material that is characterized by the small rings and picots, or loops, that both decorate the work and keep the rings together. Ladies' handkerchiefs, dresser scarves, and linens all had edging sewn on them. They added lace to dresses, baby clothes, shirts, undergarments, and several other items where lace is desired. Tatting was used to create whole caps, scarves, tablecloths, and other objects.

During the American Revolutionary War, the art temporarily faded out of style in America, but it was going strong in Europe. In Appenzell and St. Gallen, Switzerland, numerous tatting factories were established during this period. Later, some also appeared in Germany's Plauen. Many women were employed by these factories to produce the handmade lace tatting. Even one yard of lace required hours to make, because this was a tedious work.

During the Victorian era, tatting regained its level of popularity. Most young girls in Europe and America learnt how to tat from their mothers or grandmothers. In the one-room country schools of the Ozarks, females and occasionally even boys, learned to tat. Some girls learnt how to tat since all the females had to learn. They all got a shuttle and started. It was a great time for them. They didn't exactly do the first few stitches correctly.

In the country school where most activities and projects included all students old enough to participate, some of the girls learnt from their elder brother who was one of the boys who learnt how to do tatting with the other kids. "When their brother started tatting at home, they became interested in the craft, they pleaded with them to show them, and they always did.

After The Great World War 1 in many places, tatting, like most Victorian things were excessively old fashioned for the modern progressive lady. Despite the fact that many older women continued to make lace and even teach it in country Ozarks schools, tatting's national popularity declined once more. However, tatting is experiencing yet another revival right now thanks to the new interest in all things handmade. Even though it appears to be difficult, once the basic concept is grasped, it is not difficult. It has great benefits and the cost is very low.

Since the 1700s, the materials used in tatting have remained unchanged. Everything needed are thread and a shuttle. Tatting lace can be made with threads of varying sizes and types. Although any thread, string, or yarn can be used for tatting, fine white cottons have traditionally been the thread of choice. The thread typically ranges from very fine tatting crochet thread in size 70 to pearl cotton in sizes like #5 or #3.

The most delicate lace for edgings is made with the finer thread, which is harder to work with. The heavier thread, best for beginners to learn with, is used for baby covers, purses and other more durable items.

The shuttle is a simple, small, and portable handheld device used to wound the thread. It has a flat oblong shape to effectively pass, under and through the thread during the process of making the knots or stitches, in tatting. It has a point on one end that can be used to catch mistakes and join tatting rings together like a crochet hook. Shuttles are exceptionally cheap and last for like eternity. Ivory, bone, or wood were the most common materials for the early shuttles were made from, though wood shuttles were less pliable than other types. A tatting shuttle can now be purchased made of a variety of materials, including tortoise shell, steel, bone, and plastic. Some are elaborately designed while others are exceptionally plain. They vary in sizes from three to five inches long, with the bigger ones being used for the bigger thread. Smaller ones are easier in Handling. A part of the mental shuttles do have removable bobbin on which the thread can be wound easily with a sewing machine, this method can save the tedious job of hand winding. This kind of shuttle is very useful, but beginners should use a plastic shuttle because steel shuttles can get complicated. Wind the thread on the shuttle by initially tying the thread through the hole in the center of the shuttle and winding it full, however not beyond the edge of the shuttle.

Terms used in Tatting

A few terms used in the following instructions need to be familiarized with by beginners before they can begin the actual art of tatting.

- **Circle Thread** – this is the thread wound around the left hand during tatting.
- **Shuttle Thread** - The shuttle thread is the threads

that extend from the shuttle to the left hand.

- **Double Stitches** - Tatting starts with a double stitch, which is the fundamental stitch. It comprises of a first part and a second part which are half stitches or knots.
- **Picot** - One of the French terms remained despite the change in the French name for tatting. The term picot is French for point. Picots give tatting its delicate decorative effect by creating small loops between double stitches.

- **Ring** - A collection of pulled-in picots and stitches form the ring.

Chapter Two

Hand Positions

Mastering how to hold the shuttle and thread is the first step in learning to tat. Even though at first some of the positions may seem unnecessary, a little practice will show why it is important to follow instructions carefully. The following hand positions provide the greatest speed and efficiency. Use a mirror on the photographs and drawings to demonstrate positions if you are left-handed.

- Unwind around 15 inches out of the shuttle. Grab the shuttle's flat sides in a horizontal position with the point toward the left while holding it in the right hand. The thread should always come from the opposite side of the shuttle from you, in the back.

Holding the shuttle thread and shuttle

- Grab about three inches of the loose end of the thread, in between the left thumb and index finger. The loose end ought to dangle down.

- Pass the thread over the middle ring, and little fingers of the left hand by spreading them out.

Wrap around the left hand's fingers in.

- Securely grasp the thread between the thumb and index finger as you wrap it around your hand to form a circle. The result is what we will refer to as the "circle thread."

Place your hand between your left thumb and finger. Wrap over right little finger.

- Adjust the circle thread so that the fingers are slightly spread out and comfortable.
- Keeping the right and left hands level equal, unwind the shuttle thread to about 10 inches. The shuttle

thread is the thread that comes from the shuttle.

- Reach the bottom of the shuttle thread with the little finger at your right hand (or little finger and ring if more comfortable) and hold the thread to control the tension.

Basic Double Stitch

- To make the primary portion of the double stitch, keeping hands ready, move the shuttle towards the left hand and slip the shuttle point first under the shuttle thread below the circle thread between the index and middle finger. Bring it back over the circle thread and down inside the circle shaped by the shuttle thread. Allow the threads to slide between the shuttle and your finger or thumb as you pass it under and over the threads. After inserting the shuttle into the loop, release the little finger's grip on the shuttle thread and draw it out, but do not tighten it.(as shown below)

Under the circle thread, slip shuttle.

- First makes a single hitch around the circle thread, (as in the picture below) however the hitch should be tightened on the shuttle thread.
- The second step is crucial and may need to be done multiple times before you get it right. During this step, keep the shuttle

thread taut. Drop the three left-hand fingers that have been holding the circle thread taut while still holding it securely with the thumb and index finger. Now, give the shuttle thread a slight jerk to tighten it. (as shown in the second picture below) This development ought to put the bitch or stitch on the shuttle thread.

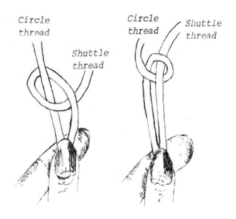

Join the circle thread in a single hitch. Drop the left hand fingers and tighten the shuttle thread, putting hitch on shuttle thread.

- Pull slightly downward on the taut shuttle thread by raising the middle finger of your left hand to move the stitch down the thread to your thumb and index fingers, (as shown below).

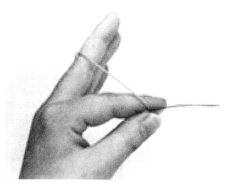

Draw the first half of double stitch downward between thumb and index finger.

- Repeat Step 1 to create the second half of the double stitch. This time, place the shuttle over the circle thread, bring it back under the circle thread, and then pass it through the loop that this is created.

Go over the circle thread and under the shuttle thread to create a second single hitch, but do not pull too tight.

- Relax the left hand's three fingers and let the shuttle

thread fall off the right hand's little finger.
- To attach the stitch to the shuttle thread, sharply jerk the shuttle thread taut like you did in Step 2.

Relax the left hand's fingers and pull the shuttle thread taut. This ought to put it on the shuttle thread.

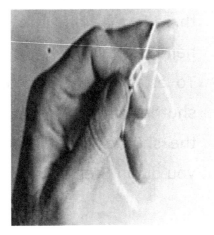

To complete the double stitch, pull the two single hitches together.

- Slid the loop into place against the first half stitch with your middle finger raised. The second half of the double stitch is complete with this.

Note: Check to see if the stitch will slip on the shuttle thread to verify that it was done correctly. If it doesn't, you'll have to either cut it off or pick out the knot and start over.

- Since the stitches are placed on the shuttle thread and subsequently slip on the thread, to make the circle larger as work progresses, unwind the thread out from the shuttle and get the thread through.

Chapter Three

Rings and Picots

Every tatted design has a variety of rings and picots. The design is built on the rings, and the picots, which are used to join the pieces together and give tatting its delicate look and dainty. The basic ring with four picots is the subject of these instructions. Numerous designs employ more picots to create a lacier appearance.

- To start the first ring make four double stitch.
- Next, create the first half of a double stitch, stopping about 1/4 inch from the

previous double stitch as you slide it into position. The spacing's of these picots is your choice. The fact that they are all spaced equally for uniform design is most important. To keep this stitch in place, you might need to put your thumb and index finger on it.
- Complete the twofold join.

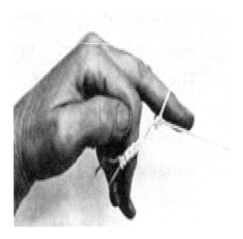

To make a double stitch, keep the first half of the stitch 1/4 inch away from the last double stitch. Complete the line.

- Slide the entire stitch in opposition to the four initial double stitches. A picot is the small loop that forms when thread is left between the last two double stitches.

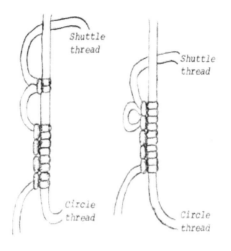

Slide the whole stitch down close to the last sets of stitches. A small loop known as a "picot" will be the result from this.

- Perform three additional double stitches and one more picot.

- Keep doing this until you have three picots and three double stitches at the end.
- Holding the stitches safely between the left hand index finger and thumb, drop the circle thread from the left hand and tension the shuttle thread tight with the goal that both the last and first stitches meet to forming a ring.

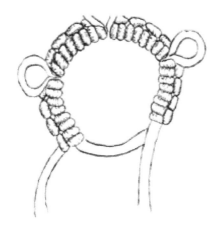

To create a "ring," drop the circle thread and slide down all three picots and double stitches.

Joinings

- To create the second ring and joinings, wrap the thread around the left hand so that it is in position for the next ring. You observe

the recently completed ring is now hanging down with the end thread.
- Make four double stitches 1/4 inch away from the ring recently made.
- Similar to a crochet stitch, insert the shuttle's point through the previous ring's last picot and pull the shuttle's point under the circle thread to catch the thread.

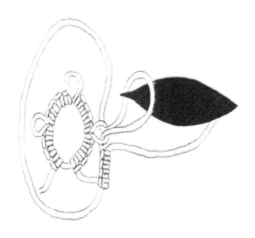

Insert the shuttle's point through the previous ring's last picot. Get the shuttle through the loop formed, as you would in a crochet join.

- With circle thread still wound around your hand, get the thread through the picot until the new loop formed is huge enough for

the whole shuttle to pass through it.
- Pull the shuttle thread taut and draw the shuttle through the loop.
- To make the circle thread, raise the middle finger of your left hand. This creates the first half of the new double stitch by joining the first part of the second ring to the first part.
- Finish the double stitch.
- Complete the new ring by starting with three double stitches and a picot, three double stitches and a picot ending with four double stitches as done earlier.

- Perform this method for each subsequent ring. This method shows the way to make a series of rings typically used on handkerchiefs, pillowcases, and so on. To be trimmed.

Ball and Shuttle Threads

After learning how to create rings, you might wish to make a more complicated pattern of rings and chains. One shuttle thread is wound in a complete circle around the left hand to create the rings, which are made by connecting the picots as mentioned above. Chains are the scallop loops beneath the rings and are made with halfway wound thread around the hand.

It is necessary to use two working threads shuttle thread and a thread on a ball, when rings and chains appear in the same design. With two threads having two colors is also possible.

- To start tie the end of the ball thread to the end of the shuttle thread, making one continues thread. Between the left hand's index finger and thumb, hold knot. On the shuttle thread, make the first ring. Put the first stitch very close to the knot as could be expected.

- Once the ring is completed, you can begin making the chain. The ring should be turned over so that the place where it is joined (the base) is at the top. Place it in the space in between your index finger and thumb. The term for this is reverse work.
- Stretch the ball thread over the back of the fingers of the left hand similarly with the way is done with the circle thread, however rather than making a total circle, wind it around the little finger to hold it and to control the tension.

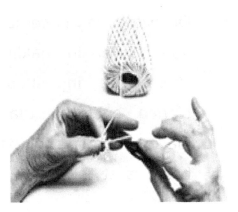

Wind the ball thread around the little fingers of the left hand and the ring to control the tension.

- With shuttle and shuttle thread create stitches on the circle thread (which presently is the ball string). Place the first stitch as close to the newly formed ring as possible. Form a chain by creating a series of stitches.

These can be done in multiple ways. For a simple pattern, one chain requires four stitches, one picot, and four stitches.

Make a series of double stitch. Make one picot. Repeat with the same number of double stitches earlier done.
- When the chain section is completed, pull the stitches

together and put the ball thread down.

- Turn the work around so that the shuttle thread comes from the top, (reverse it).

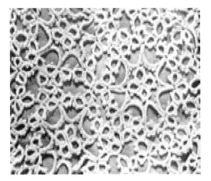

Beautiful things are made of tiny tatted stitches.

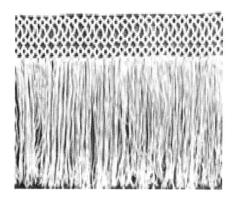

The extra-long picots used to create this scarf's fringe were cut after being made.

Tatted purse done.

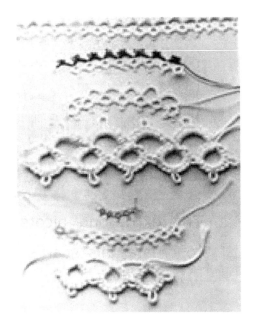

Stitches of varying sizes are created by the various sizes of thread.

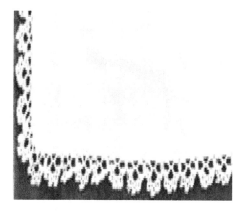

Tatted lace is more frequently used on handkerchiefs.

- Create a second ring by employing shuttle thread as the circle thread. As before, join the rings.
- Make the desired rings and chains by reversing the work and using shuttle and ball threads alternately.

Reverse the work in other to make a new ring.

Splicing and Ends

When you need to add more thread, tie a strong, flat knot as close to the end of a ring or chain as possible. However, avoid cutting off the ends too close to the ring or chain to prevent the stitches from pulling out. All splices must be tied at this point because the stitches will not slide over a knot.

Whip stitch all loose ends to the wrong side of the work with a needle and matching color sewing thread for a neater finish and to prevent tatting from unraveling.

For a finished look, whip stitch the ends.

The fundamental tatting design should be doable if you follow all of these steps. After mastering the rings, picots, and chains, you might want to move on to other tatting supplies in a variety of designs and variations. However, keep in mind that mastery requires time and practice. Then, at that point, you, as well, can agree with me that, "It's simple once you get it mastered."

Made in the USA
Monee, IL
23 December 2024